DATE DUE

This Is What I Want to Be

Construction Worker

Heather Miller

Heinemann Library
Chicago, Illinois

©2003 Reed Educational & Professional Publishing
Published by Heinemann Library,
an imprint of Reed Educational & Professional Publishing
Chicago, IL

Customer Service 888-454-2279
Visit our website at www.heinemannlibrary.com

Designed by Sue Emerson, Heinemann Library
Printed and bound in the United States by Lake Book Manufacturing, Inc.

07 06 05 04 03
10 9 8 7 6 5 4 3 2 1

Library of Congress Cataloging-in-Publication Data
Miller, Heather.
      Construction worker / Heather Miller.
          p. cm. — (This is what I want to be)
Includes index.
Summary: An introduction to the educational background, equipment, clothing, and various duties of a construction worker.
      ISBN: 1-4034-0365-1 (HC), 1-4034-0587-5 (Pbk.)
      1. Building—Juvenile literature. 2. Construction workers—Juvenile literature.
      [1. Building. 2. Construction workers. 3. Occupations.] I. Title.
      TH149.M55 2002
      624'.092—dc21

                              2001008132

Acknowledgments
The author and publishers are grateful to the following for permission to reproduce copyright material:

p. 4 G. Brad Lewis/Visuals Unlimited; p. 5R Bill Miles/Corbis Stock Market; pp. 5L, 8, 11R Phil Martin/Heinemann Library; p. 6 Alex L. Fradkin/PhotoDisc; p. 7 Ted Curtin/Stock Boston; p. 9 Chuck Keeler Jr./Corbis Stock Market; p. 10L PhotoDisc; p. 10R Inga Spence/Visuals Unlimited; p. 11L John Boykin/Index Stock Imagery/PictureQuest; p. 12 Arnulf Husmo/Stone/Getty Images; p. 13 Janet Gill/Stone/Getty Images; p. 14 Andy Levin/Photo Researchers, Inc.; p. 15 Dean Conger/Corbis; p. 16 Bob Daemmrich/Stock Boston; p. 17 Kevin A. Byron/Bruce Coleman Inc.; p. 18L Jeff Greenberg/ Visuals Unlimited; p. 18R John Burke/Index Stock Imagery, Inc.; p. 19 Ralf Gerard/Stone/Getty Images; p. 20 Jock Montgomery/Bruce Coleman Inc.; p. 21 Edmond Van Hoorick/PhotoDisc; p. 23 (row 1, L-R) Andy Levin/Photo Researchers, Inc., Ted Curtin/Stock Boston, Andy Levin/Photo Researchers, Inc., Corbis Stock Market; p. 23 (row 2, L-R) Ralf Gerard/Stone/Getty Images, Ted Curtin/Stock Boston, Ralf Gerard/Stone/Getty Images, Dean Conger/Corbis; p. 23 (row 3, L-R) John Burke/Index Stock Imagery, Inc., Phil Martin/Heinemann Library, Arnulf Husmo/Stone/Getty Images, Ted Curtin/Stock Boston; p. 23 (row 4, L-R) Sue Emerson/Heinemann Library, Chuck Keeler Jr./Corbis Stock Market, Andy Levin/Photo Researchers, Inc., PhotoDisc

Cover photograph by Bill Miles/Corbis Stock Market
Photo research by Scott Braut

Every effort has been made to contact copyright holders of any material reproduced in this book. Any omissions will be rectified in subsequent printings if notice is given to the publisher.

Special thanks to our advisory panel for their help in the preparation of this book:

Eileen Day, Preschool Teacher
Chicago, IL

Ellen Dolmetsch, MLS
Wilmington, DE

Kathleen Gilbert,
Second Grade Teacher
Austin, TX

Sandra Gilbert,
Library Media Specialist
Houston, TX

Angela Leeper,
Educational Consultant
North Carolina Department
of Public Instruction
Raleigh, NC

Pam McDonald, Reading Teacher
Winter Springs, FL

Melinda Murphy,
Library Media Specialist
Houston, TX

Some words are shown in bold, **like this.**
You can find them in the picture glossary on page 23.

Contents

What Do Construction Workers Do?

Construction workers build things.

They build roads, houses, and **skyscrapers**.

Some construction workers drive big machines.

Others hammer nails or cut wood.

What Special Jobs Do Construction Workers Do?

Construction workers do not always build new things.

Sometimes they take things down.

wrecking ball   excavator   crane

A **crane** driver swings a **wrecking ball**.

An **excavator** lifts the pieces away.

What Do Construction Workers Wear?

Construction workers wear clothes that keep them safe.

This worker is wearing **goggles** and gloves.

Construction workers wear **helmets.**

They also wear strong boots.

What Tools Do Construction Workers Use?

Construction workers pound with hammers.

They twist with **wrenches.**

cement

Construction workers dig
with shovels.

They use **trowels** to spread cement.

Where Do Construction Workers Work?

Construction workers work wherever things need to be built.

This construction worker is building an **oil rig** in the ocean.

Some construction workers work in big cities.

Others work along roads.

Do Construction Workers Work in Other Places?

beam

Some construction workers work high above the ground.

They put up **beams** for tall buildings.

Some construction workers work underground.

They build **tunnels.**

When Do Construction Workers Work?

Construction workers can work at any time.

They often start working early in the morning.

Construction workers sometimes work at night.

They work for many hours.

What Kinds of Construction Workers Are There?

Carpenters work with wood.

Ironworkers work with metal.

Masons build with **bricks**.

They build walls and **chimneys**.

How Do People Become Construction Workers?

Some construction workers learn as they work.

They practice using tools.

Other people go to special schools.

They learn how buildings are
put together.

Quiz

Can you remember what these things are called?

Look for the answers on page 24.

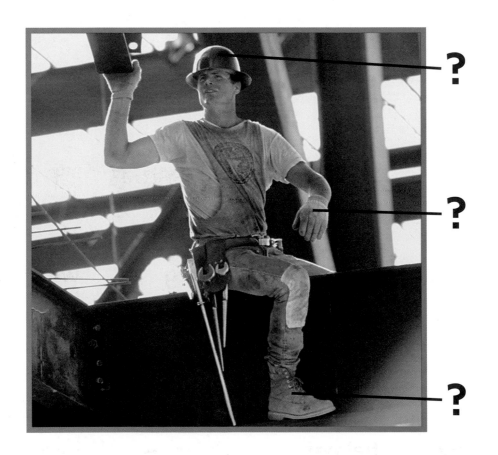

?

?

?

Picture Glossary

beam
page 14

crane
page 7

ironworker
page 18

trowel
page 11

brick
page 19

excavator
page 7

mason
page 19

tunnel
page 15

carpenter
page 18

goggles
page 8

oil rig
page 12

wrecking ball
page 7

chimney
page 19

helmet
page 9

skyscraper
page 4

wrench
page 10

23

Note to Parents and Teachers

Reading for information is an important part of a child's literacy development. Learning begins with a question about something. Help children think of themselves as investigators and researchers by encouraging their questions about the world around them. Each chapter in this book begins with a question. Read the question together. Look at the pictures. Talk about what you think the answer might be. Then read the text to find out if your predictions were correct. Think of other questions you could ask about the topic, and discuss where you might find the answers. Assist children in using the picture glossary and the index to practice new vocabulary and research skills.

Index

Answers to quiz on page 22

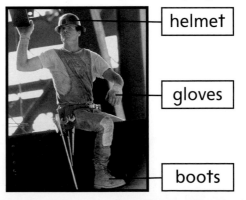

helmet

gloves

boots